W0115447

DARK UNDER KIGANDA STARS

DARK UNDER KIGANDA STARS

Lilah Hegnauer

AUSABLE PRESS
2005

Cover art: scanned cloth from Tanzania

Design and composition by Ausable Press.
The type is Adobe Jenson.
Cover design by Rebecca Soderholm.

Published by
AUSABLE PRESS
1026 HURRICANE ROAD, KEENE NY 12942
www.ausablepress.org

Distributed by
CONSORTIUM BOOK SALES & DISTRIBUTION
1045 WESTGATE DRIVE
SAINT PAUL MN 55114
800-283-3572
651-379-5334
FAX: 651-917-6406

The Acknowledgments appear on page 117 and constitute
a continuation of the copyrights page.

© 2005 by Lilah Hegnauer
All rights reserved
Manufactured in the United States of America
First Edition

Library of Congress Cataloging-in-Publication Data
Hegnauer, Lilah, 1982—
Dark under Kiganda stars : poems / by Lilah Hegnauer. — 1st ed.
p. cm.
ISBN 1-931337-23-3 (pbk. : alk. paper)
1. Uganda—Poetry. 2. Education—Poetry. 3. Women teachers—Poetry. I. Title.
PS3608.E35D37 2005
811'.6
2004030346

for Herman

Pronunciation Guide

I. *SEEING THROUGH*

II. *THE FIREFLY*

III. *CONSTANT*

PRONUNCIATION GUIDE *for the* LUGANDA LANGUAGE

Ki is pronounced chi with a short i sound, as in *Kiganda* (Chi-GAN-da) and *Kigongo* (Chi-GONG-go).

Kya is pronounced cha, as in *Kyatebbe* (Cha-ka-TE-be).

Ky is chi with a long i sound, as in *Kyeune* (Chi-YOO-nae).

When the letters 'n' and 'm' are followed by a consonant, it is pronounced not as 'en' but almost as a humming sound running into the other letter, as in *Nkizire*, *Ntambi*, and *Mpologoma*.

Often, if a name or word ends with a vowel, the sound is dropped off or shortened and softened, as in *Abassi*, *Kizito*, and *Musini*.

When a consonant or vowel is doubled, the sound become stronger and longer, as in *Kawooya*, which is not pronounced with the 'oo' sound as in pool, but simply a more stressed version of the long 'o' sound.

The penultimate syllable receives the stress, as in *Turinaruhangha* (Too-rhi-na-roo-HAN-gha).

I.

SEEING THROUGH

HEADSHAPES

Before I knew their names, before I knew which were my students
and which were stealing in from other classes, I used
their Christian names, Muslim names, simple names.

Muhammad and Caroline and Margaret in the first bench,
Davis and Allan and Robert in the second—until I called on
        Davis
as Maureen. The same hair, same shirt, same color,

I couldn't tell boys from girls without bending like a pecking hen
to see the skirts and trousers. I started looking at headshapes—
how far and round the head curves above the ears, how low or long

the forehead is, how broad or sharp the bridge of the nose, how far
the lobes of the ears reach. Do the cheeks come out much in a
        smile,
and does the skin around the chin tighten towards those earlobes?

How soft is the indent at the temples and does it meet the high
        cheekbones?
Ntambi's forehead shows muscles above his eyebrows, Musini's
        head
is more pointed than flat but just slightly. I stopped calling out

Jane and Lillian and Joseph; Mukabalisa and Mugalula and
        Amanyire
are the names they use with one another—spoken affirmation
of Ssenono's vein running barefaced, bisecting his forehead, and
        the base
of his skull curving on the same plane as the backs of his earlobes.

TEACH ANYTHING

Teach anything, the headmaster told me;
he didn't return for five weeks. Clueless
as a gift chicken, I slowly learned
our lessons: they didn't know about

the slave trade, Martin Luther King, snow,
informal greetings, Shakespeare. Everything
was new, the world of English burst forth
tart on their palates: verbs, nouns,

conjugation of tenses. Amanyire whispered
to Mukabalisa, "Whatever you choose to claim
of me is always yours, *nkwagala*;" I dropped
my jaw. My hands and their papers dropped.

English infiltrated their romance. I can't
understand my body turning toward them,
turning away, turning again, and finally away;
English, Luganda, they're speaking Luzungu.

I learn each evening, roasting maize on charcoal,
language doesn't matter when it comes to love.
Like yellow kernels taking on the heat,
gradually we all want to be printed upon.

If I could sink myself into this ink and write myself
onto a page I would lie down in what they taught me
about iambs: walk under a full moon to the latrine—don't
light the lantern, leave it next to the sleeper.

Go later in the month when the moon is a hair, don't
light the lantern, fumble to the pit and back into bed.
Teach anything. Print the way upon your mind
until it's all sensory, all footpath-thin, all charted loam.

SEEING THROUGH

I'm at the blackboard watching Mukabalisa
slip Amanyire's beads off his wrist; they don't know

I spy her playfully put the beads back on him,
holding his thumb with one hand, rubbing her other up his arm,

around his head; Mukabalisa puts his beads on when I
walk in to teach and takes them off as I walk out.

Ntambi now sits between the hips of Ayebazibwe
and Nakalyango; he leans on Ayebazibwe as he had

with Kawooya before his beans came ready to harvest.
Bursar sends nineteen home for school fees; after he leaves,

they wait and trickle back in without looking at me.
We're making lists of synonyms—lists for friend, mother,

happy, sad—Amanyire starts a list for 'want' and another for 'attract.'
When the rain comes in the late morning, he wants a list for echo.

MILK

On break, between Senior IV and Senior III,
I was hunch-backed, grading papers in silence
with Madam Esther, sharing hotcakes and
fried cassava. With dim light in the office,
when Kyambadde came in, I didn't see
the thermos of milk; I didn't see his hands,
still wet from rinsing off chalk;
I couldn't see his eyes, but his head was
cocked to one side. He set the thermos before me.
His mother had sent milk for me.

Madam Esther didn't look up; the thermos
was not to share. Kyambadde left, and I
let the thermos sit there until Madam Esther
reached to the cupboard, pulled out a metal mug,
and went on with her papers. I released
the cap, let the steam hiss out, and
poured milk, plopping foully;
Madam Esther didn't look up. Kyambadde
came back, eager to see me drinking milk.

I took the mug to my lips and sucked in
three lumps, squishing them between my
back teeth before swallowing the flattened
bits of curdle; Kyambadde smiled,
lifted the thermos to check for more milk.
No! he exclaimed and poured for me.
I drank it all down, pushed my papers aside

for Kyambadde to sit and tell me
about Rwanda where his wife is from.
That night I was hunched-backed in my room.
Dinner came back up, but Kyambadde
sat with me in the dim light the next morning,
resting his elbows on the chair back, letting
his dangling hands lift and fall
with each *"ayi, bambi"* and *"bambi, bambi."*

ON NOT CANING MY STUDENTS

Caning is effective punishment
for not coming prepared to debate,

for tardiness, for failing an exam,
for disrupting class, for disrespecting a teacher,

for not sweeping the classroom,
for not handing in homework,

for talking out of turn, for not having school fees.
Ugandan children learn through their backsides.

I hate the crack across the backs of their thighs
I hate seeing the muscles in men-students'

clenched jaws and in the teachers' sinewy forearms,
I hate the shallow hiccoughing breaths, I hate

the girls' screams, but I never say anything.
I'm not a source of enlightenment.

I'm sickened by teaching this language.
Gerald tells me I have become this switch

in his life, I am his pulse; like a stick
I want to be splintered, burned, stripped into

fibers and woven to usefulness, but
all I am doing is not caning my students.

AGNUS DEI

For Nakalyango Fildah getting excited about iambs
and tapping her hand on her desk when she speaks.

For Kibirige Jackson failing the vocab quiz
but making me laugh: the word 'ordination'
comes from the word 'ordinate,' 'ordinate'
comes from the word 'order' which means
arranging something. 'Monk' is a name of an
animal (wild animal) eg. monkeys. Couldn't
remember 'statuesque' but made this
sentence: "I want to refine my body
so I can become like a 'structure.'"

For Bamwine Coleb, Mugisha Elisa, Ssennono Vincent, Ntambi
        Muhammad,
Nkizire Robertson, Ssemakula Novanto, Ntege Charles, Kawooya
        Davis

For Kyeyune Emmanuel wanting to be
an English teacher, coming to the blackboard
passionate not noticing a three inch pock
writing the chalk right into that hole, sending it
to pieces, bits landing all over the floor.

For Musini Eridad with argyle socks calling himself
Mafia writing a story about a girl befriending
a seagull and giving it food because it can't dig for itself.

For Amazalakufa Douglas, Mukasa Ahmed, Biira Maureen,
        Ssempijja Amos,
Nabakiibi Justine, Nabulime Annette, Mugalula Lillian,
        Mukabalisa Jane

For Happy Winnie and Peterson Laughter
(their parents wanted English names). Happy born
on Christmas, Laughter born during white ant season.

For Ssettuba Godfrey pronouncing 'she' as 'see'
getting jeers as he reads a story about his
sister's wedding; he still reads every time.
For Mudangha Andrew, twenty-two loving casual greetings
and shouts mornings from the back, "Howdy, Madam!"

For Ssekitoleko Edward, Bukenya Kalimu, Ssembwayo Achilles,
Ssekabira Robert, Battira Abaasi, Kizito Jamil, Friday Gelsom
        Besigye

For Nnannyonga Effrance crying silently after I turn
from writing the exam on the blackboard, no pen
no paper and caned already by Madam Esther
for tardiness, tears come harder when I
give her my good black pen and paper.

For Nandugwa Harriet and Haluvubi Zabiibah
unprepared to debate and caned—4 sticks each
Ayebazibwe Caroline walking 4 kilometers and

being late and not sweeping caned by Madam Esther
3 sticks on the first hit the stick broke; she fetched
another to finish. Harunah Nseko and Zirimenya Allan
fighting in the schoolyard during lunch caned by
Madam Esther—7 sticks each in front of the student body.

For Kyambadde Costant, Nnamuddu Salima, Ssenjako Rhajab,
        Jombwe Siraje,
Hassan Mubiru, Nyama Noah, Nampeewo Margaret,
        Ndayambaze Mesach,
Ssagala Kizito, Ssegawa Lufunsi, Nnabunnya Naggayi Sarah,
    Mugabirwe John

For Amanyire Joseph, seventeen, shocked when I share
Wole Soyinka with the class, and can't believe we
read African poets; his father is 89 years old,
his mother is 54; he informed me that
Baganda men are potent their whole lives through.

For a student, fourteen, raped coming home from school
by a boda-boda man. She lives at the convent.
She and her girl baby have sores in their mouths,
the infant a ring of lesions under the fold in her neck.

For Nankanja Betty, Kyambadde Sham, Ssentamu Tadeo, Monday
        Richard,
Byalugaba Posiano, Muwonge Posiano, Male Benard, Ssemwanga
        Joseph
Ssentiba Fred, Kugonza Barnabas, Katende Wakim, Nakku
        Regina

For Kigongo Moses five feet tall,
writing stories about angels and mothers,
the youngest of nine with eight older sisters.

For Turinaruhanga, whose name means
"people are created to give glory to God"
and Byamukama, whose name means
"I give praise to the Lord."

PROVERB I: CHEWING THORNS

I ask my students to write a poem trying iambs and alliteration.
Kigongo asks what it should be about, Kyeune tells him
to write about the *muzungu* teacher with a dimple in her right
       cheek
whose backlit skirt shows the outline of her legs
(I only know he said this because dutiful Kigongo translated).

I wonder why I never noticed the sheer qualities of this linen.
What else haven't I wondered enough about?
About Gerald shuddering every time I hold him.
About all the washing: clothes, dishes, hair,
body, face, cow's teats, with the same bar of soap.

About Gerald's low voice: *Nkwagala omwana*, honey;
where did he learn English terms of endearment?
Where did he learn his love for women—gentle
and transparent—eight sisters and a mother with a voice?

About Amanyire laughing at Friday Besigye for
not having shoes; he's getting quieter, sitting further back
each day. About virgin land and raped women,
caned children and men holding hands, whole milk
and cassava flour. Those who eat thorns know how to chew them.

AVOIDANCE

Narrow wooden signs nailed to jackfruit trees in the primary
     school yard
advise in bold black letters "Avoid Early Sex" and "Avoid Early
     Marriage."
Fildah gives a speech about her sister, Rose, and lowers her eyes
     and voice
telling us Rose is in Kampala selling *chapats* to taxi riders.

The class riles her as she ended the speech, "is she missing teeth
     too?"
"is she lame?" Ntambi asks from the front row, "wasn't your sister
     raped?"
The class explodes, chatter and taunts, Kawooya gives Ntambi a
     toothy smile,
Nseko leans back onto the desk behind him and extends his legs
     into the tight aisle.
Fildah can't get back to her desk. Ssembwayo says, "yeah, she
     prostituted herself."

It all comes suddenly and Fildah is just standing there; I don't
     know what to say.
I kick Nseko's legs out of the aisle, let Filah retreat to her spot next
     to Ayebazibwe.
I stand before them utterly dumb, knees back into their overex-
     tended position,
wondering where did this came from and feeling the blood rise to
     my ears.

"Before you ask a question, you must raise your hand and wait,"
        I tell the class.
How do I do this? "Rape (the class goes silent) is a tragedy and
        men are to blame.
For tomorrow, your speech topic is 'how I plan to protect myself
        against rape' for
the women and 'how I plan to protect my sisters from rape' for the
        men."

I walk home brooding on what went wrong, how I let the class
        beat on Fildah.
I brood about the assignment. What if a Kiganda woman broke
        her rapist's nose?
Does that mean she won't pay later? Doesn't "Avoid Early Sex"
        mean
"kick him hard and run"? Are men to blame? I don't know, I don't
        know, *se' mani.*

HUT HURT HAT HEART
(or HUT HUT HUT HUT)

When I wrote them on the blackboard
and said them aloud, a collective breath
was gathered by the class and they tried
to imitate me. They invoked the image of parrots

with something new to practice, and I was angry
with myself, I second-guessed this lesson;
it seems I'm always guessing: can I do this?
Is this right? If hurt is a hat, do I sin in telling them

another way? I love the fluid sounds and the tonal ok
I love the music of five and six syllable names
Turinaruhanga, Byalugaba, Ayebazibwe,
but I love them as novelty, not as the bone-

resonating *Luzungu* words that fill my mouth
in so many segments of hard and soft, of sanguine
presaging about rainfall and crop yield, of the
palliating pedant with questions she almost wishes

wouldn't rise. But they do because hurt and hat
go hand on head; they go walking together
to the tops of hills and fall painfully
bud over bird back down again. Hut and heart

boil porridge together in the mornings when the fog
hangs on the southern hills. They do, they do;
these two tongues twist like loosening
banana fibers in my attempts at weaving.

PROVERB II: IT IS THE GRASS

When two elephants fight,
it is the grass that gets hurt.
When Bukenya punched Zirimenya
square across the jaw
in the schoolyard during lunch,
Zirimenya's head flew right,
his neck, his shoulders, his hips,
everything turned right,
spit flew from his mouth,
tears came to rest with blood
on his open chin. Madam Esther
called an assembly, 246 students

crowded in, sweating against
each other, to watch the caning.
I sat in the teachers' office,
my toes clenched into the thick
of my feet, grading papers,
watching the hand on my watch
tick by. I try to be this living clay,
from silence that needs to grow.
I try to be this living grass,
from clay in the rainy season,
flooding season. When grass dies,
to what will rain cling and reflect?

KIGANDA WOMEN: SECONDARY SCHOOL
(Fildah with Stanley Kunitz I)

Educating women is a waste of money.
Women in secondary school find boys
and prostitute themselves. The girls are dull.
Women lack focus and ambition. Women should
only be educated enough to raise their dowry
enough to be intelligent conversationalists
for their husbands. School is for men. Jobs
are for men. Women should produce children.

Education leads to rebellion and a lack of morals.
Fildah, what was it that drew you to him?
Was it the phrase *drives you up the wall* or the notion
of the body as borrowed dust? Or was it his phrase
utility took fantasy for wife that made you
come to me after class, asking to borrow the book?
What was it that led me to give it to you so freely,
thrusting it into your hands, telling you to enjoy it,

bring it back on Monday, keep it forever,
I can get another? Fildah, you've set yourself apart,
I'm sorry, you're turning inward, turning away
from duty, watching your own mind grow;
Fildah, don't let me step into your mind,
your place. I'll change it. School is for you,
jobs are for you, lay your mind in the book,
your lost clarity, my phantasm of utility.

FILDAH WITH STANLEY KUNITZ II

Night is coming, but Maama knows where I am.
She tries to let me be—a girl, lonely,
the youngest with eight brothers. She finally
got her girl then Taata died. Instead of
keeping me home like she ought, she lets me
stay out, she knows I'm not anything that any boy
would want—two teeth missing from the top.
The mosquitoes are coming in from the field
and this lantern attracts them but I can't go in yet.
This is mine, the English madam let me take
her book and I'm going to stay out all night
under this mango tree. Alone. Not sharing.
Not milking, not peeling, not shelling, not cooking,
not washing, not me. Maama brought me porridge
in Taata's metal mug and I'm going to read
"Tristia" over and over, again and again—
oh, how scrawny is the language of joy.

PROVERB III: THE BLIND MOTHER

A girl whose mother is blind
dances and looks at the sun.

My dream of Fildah:
she is with me in America.
All her teeth are in her mouth.
She swishes and spits clear water
fast on the ground while
counting her change at the bus stop.

Her eyelids close, full moons,
brown and taut against her skin,

blinding her to that mother she left.
A girl whose mother is blind
does not have time to dance and dance;
she measures the days by the sun.
So I watch her and every cent of
this cost, that every eye and slowing heart

will know the midnight, the corner stop,
the dry and rainy seasons of Kiganda's sun.

WALKING WITH JUDE AND THE CHICKEN

It was live, a gift from the headmaster. My students came out of
       the classroom
laughing wide-mouthed as the headmaster handed me the chicken
and I tried to take it and hold it as he had, cradled under one arm
       like a *paw-paw*,
but the chicken struck its wings out in the passing and pumped its
       tied legs.

I spooked and pushed it away without meaning to, tears breached
       the rims of my eyes,
I couldn't control that either, "thank you, the sun is too bright."
Jude slid the chicken from the headmaster's arm to his own
and directed me with a glance at the road—I could leave.

A goat, no bigger than the chicken, tied to a cassava tree in the
       field
across from the primary school yard crying from loneliness.
Two girls in pink dresses, hair shaved, arms linked,
heads bent conversation. Jude next to me silent with the chicken.

A woman with a full bunch of green matoke bananas on her head
       and
an infant tied to her back, its head nestled between her shoulder
       blades.
A man slapping his feet as he weaves down the path from the
       tonto spot
up the hill calling "Beautiful *Nnyabo*! Beautiful *Nnyabo*!"

I don't know how to communicate, how to bend my head close to
        a friend's
with my quiet voice, but I try to fold myself in—
Kabooi tied the back legs of the cow to keep her from kicking as I
        milked,
but he still takes over because it'd be dawn before we had porridge

if I kept milking. Desire. Desire will get me there—let me take the
        chicken again;
again let me milk the ornery cow. I swear this time I won't forget
        to kneel,
I can make my hands do work; when the goat is grown I will
take the chicken—live, a gift—and you won't notice my white
        hands.

PROVERB IV: A PROBLEM SHARED

A problem shared
is a problem half solved—
the introduction
Ntambi gave his letter
as he thrust it at me.

Asking nothing, I take
the letter and read
walking home for lunch.
Please, he writes, my
grandfather has died,
I cannot support myself.

I've always liked the sound
of breaking a book's binding.
Cracking it open, hearing
the snap as its spine
is quelled open to a
favorite passage.

A problem cracked
open near its core,
a problem laid flat,
will never close properly
again; those loved books
give and give and open,
surefire to the spine-break.

PROVERB V: NOSE AND EYES

Nose and eyes, was the extent
Ntambi told me before writing
the rest: now in Uganda
they are immunizing children
six months to eighteen years
against measles. All things are
growing, rains have come.
Even me, I'm growing up now.
I'm fifty-three kilos. I'm sixteen
years, one month, and seven days old.
I encourage you to concentrate
on your studies and work hard
for the betterment of your future
as well as mine. When smoke
gets into the eyes, the nose waters.

FAILURE

Sometimes they'd get restless after the second hour, shifting papers
       around,
turning their knees from side to side, trying to find comfort on the
       benches.
Sometimes they'd ask questions—does your family have a garden,
how old are you, what does 'fuck you' mean—and I know they're
       bored,
they don't want to read any more poems, they're tired and I'm
       pushing them,
there's a resonance hanging in the air when I ask Mukabalisa
to tell us about the place and purpose of violence in Soyinka's
       "Dawn."

Sometimes I'd answer their questions—they wanted to know
       about September 11th,
computers, AIDS in my country. Sometimes I'd spend a whole
       hour, everyone
could ask one question, but I'd try to tie in the last question with
       the literature.
I'd bring in pictures of my family, the girls huddled, staring at the
       blue eyes
of my youngest niece, my childhood friend's long blonde hair. Once

Zirimenya slipped my sister's picture into his shirt pocket and left,
hands dangling at his sides, shoulder blades pressed together in
       confidence.
I wouldn't have asked for it back, but Bukenya noticed and grabbed
       at his

slack hand before he slid out. Maybe they're not tired, maybe it's me.
Maybe it's not as I usually think: Fildah slipped the book from my
      hand
as I was busy with Bukenya and Zirimenya; she opened to "Dawn."

PROVERB VI: CAUTION IS NOT COWARDICE

Caution is not cowardice;
even the ants march armed.

Ki, ki, they call, rushing
down the embankment

toward the highway
where I am walking. One has

her uniform blouse unbuttoned
to the third button, another's

socks are rolled down
into thin white goat tails.

On our way into the classroom
after lunch, Nabakiibi

stops in the doorway,
a shadow in the sunlight,

stooped over with her knee
hiked up, tugging on her socks.

Nabulime's fingers work
quickly, fitting the buttons

to their holes as she sits,
straight-backed, next to Bukenya.

Laughter wants a mock-debate
to prepare for tomorrow, Amanyire

asks if I have their papers,
but I'm thinking of Nanyonga,

her lips pursed shut
and her eyes shifting

down, left, right. This
armor makes Nabakiibi pause

in the doorway, tuck
her chin, sit and cross her
ankles away from Bukenya.

ANGEL SAINT
for Ssenono Vicent (9/1984—9/2003)

If I could choose, if it was possible, if I was worthy, if babies'
        homes weren't crowded,
if aunts and grandparents weren't overburdened and I could take it
        all back
to the point where no man had sinned, I would rather be an angel
        than a saint.

I would rather float close to God and close to men than be
        canonized by men.
I'm dying and I see a light, I'm dying and I see my creator, I'm
        dying
and the heat which fills my veins finally calls my lifelong bluffing

and I leave. Life's been so long in coming and so quick in going—
        somewhere between
watching my parents turn hollow and smelling the rainy season
        come on again
and again life must have happened because now it's stopping and I
        can't find

the part where life happened at all. Once, madam was explaining a
        sonnet and the turns
it can take at the end and the tensions its form carries and I
        thought my life is less sonnet
and more rhymed couplet—beginning, it is nearly done and
        ending, it is still being propelled.

My lantern is fading, my coal is cooling. I want to leave this world
      and find another,
not stay remembered here where only Ugandans would notice me
      looking out
from prayer cards. They'll pray and I'll have to be the mendicant
      for their

eyelid lesions and pointed ribs, their mouth sores, night sweats,
      and patching hair;
so let me be an angel, let me watch again from above. I'll stop
      begging and
start living; please give it up, please give me up, please—I want to
      go and meet them—

the saints I prayed to, the angels who watched over me, the God
      who made me
in his image. I want to see if he has shrunken muscles, too, and
      know if his mouth
grows dry in the night so he wakes swollen and cracking. I want
      this heat, this choice.

ALMOST

Almost as much as Mudangha's explanation of the vocabulary
      word 'daydream,'
almost as much as Ntambi's drawing of a monk which was a
      crocodile, almost as much as
Jude addressing the student body with, "Howdy, folks" and my
      understanding of
detoothing and *boda-boda* men, I think, on my walk up
      Mpologoma Hill

about the fog on the southern hills as I walked to school and the
      look
of mango trees at sunrise. Almost as much as the difference
      between
folks and forks and Ntambi's biting letter—please pay my school
      fees—almost as much as
I think about seeing Mukabalisa on her way home from
      Nakiganda market with

tomatoes and a green bell pepper and a wild bird of paradise
      dangling
upside down between the fingers of her left hand, I think about
      the truck driving
slowly by with rap music so loud it rumbled my stomach and the
      seat-dance
that nearly all my students broke into at the sound of his loud
      stereo.

Almost as much as I try to remember to kneel and wave with both
        hands to the
old men I pass up this trail, almost as much as I try to remember
Musini's sonnet about Venus and the decreasing moon, and
        Nkizire's essay
on why women should not be educated, I try to remember the rain
        sweeping in

the open windows like a wildfire in and out and in again with the
        wind. Almost as
good as remembering in parts or remembering anything at all—
        please don't fade—
are the half-forgotten mornings that come back to me, approaching
        the top of Mpologoma Hill.
They come, into the endurance of grace, voyages out of otherness.

II.

THE FIREFLY

BATUME

Before I was halfway across the street you charged me down waving
        hotcakes,
bony knees swinging on double hung hinges. Batume, I'm sorry
I couldn't understand you past *Oli otya* and *mwebale*; I'm sorry
your breath was rancid of tonto and *paw-paw* and I cringed
as you stepped right up to my chest. I didn't mind talking in the
        road;
I didn't notice people coming out of their leaning shops to watch
because you smiled so wide I could count your remaining teeth—
five—and your hand was so open when you extended it
I could see your thumb was arthritic and cocked toward the palm.
Your laugh stout and dense like the stomach of a pregnant sow as
we talked about—heaven help me I'll never know—I glimpsed my
        feet
as I bent in laughter and was surprised at their color—
dirty white—when I expected them brown and bare like yours.

PAIR I: ON MY KNEES

Each time I pass Batume on the path,
I fall quickly, nearly stumbling,
to my knees. Coming up, I brush the
dust from my skirt and move on.
I feel comfortable down here,
in a dress, walking slowly; even riding
sidesaddle on the parish motorcycle.

Distinct from men, I have my role.
I know I don't live here, it's not my
culture, I enjoy it as temporary, as
novelty. But this pair—this man
woman pair—is felt, and I don't mind.

A father is outside St. Matia Mulumba
with his baby girl. Holding her hands as she
stands on the ground, he coaxes her
into taking steps, his knees spring and
bend like the sooty chat in the tree above.
Another man sits near him after scything;
both are sweaty and affectionate to the girl.

PEONIES

One parishioner asks if we are sisters.
Spera smoothes her veil, turns her
pointy hips to me, traces my brows
with each thumb, her four fingers
pressing my temples. 'God took
our brows from the same womb.'
Spera's cinnamon lips pull tight
to her teeth and draw points
at each end, with soft parentheses to frame.

"Do you want children?" she asks later
while shelling beans. Tucking her veil
into itself she wants to know,
"How many? I hope they're small.
Children." The word hangs.
Running her thumbs across a dry pod,
she presses and cracks it, "I wanted children
like layers of a peony. Folds upon thickness,
generations from me; but the dower was spent."
She untucks her veil, covering her neck.

KATENDE PASSION FRUIT AND GROUNDNUTS

Grafted, a yellow to purple hybrid, the yellow
lives longer, gives more fruit, but oh, the purple
is so sweet that the compromise is worth the loss
of longevity, the only reason for our hybrid fruit—
utility took taste for wife but it makes a poor shade
as I sat plucking groundnuts with Kabooi.

When I came to help, he cleared a space on the mat
and turned his body on splayed knees to face me.
His trousers were cuffed higher than I remember,
his fingers were bent to the raw nuts, his
eyebrows thick over a disquiet face. Kabooi, they
call him or he calls himself; Cowboy, I used to say
because he tends the cows. "You are married,"

he said, with that look older men often give me,
wondering how long I'll stay and why I'm here.
I'm not marriageable, I tried to say—but am lost at
how to tell him of my own grafting; instead, I
grabbed a clump of dirt and nuts and harvested with
Kabooi deep into the evening until the sky
was a plowed mix of orange and blue.

EATING WHITE ANTS

White wings with black bodies,
they come in June, in October.
No one knows from where,
but they come up with the rain
in droves of all sizes. During
night rains, children will wake
and take lanterns to the anthills
to catch them coming out like
refugees through the borders.
Children crouch with their
sheets of paper rolled into cones
with the bottom point pinched
shut and scoop them out; when
the cone is filled, they'll fold
the top over. White ants can be sold
but most children come barefoot,
sleeves in the mud, and pick the ants
by the wings, pull off the wings
at the same time, like picking
a loose thread from a collar.
They eat white ants without waiting,
squashing the insects
between the tip of the tongue
and the roof of the mouth,
flicking the wings out like
ash or white ash, or even snow.
Farther up the same path
will be another group,

eating white ants as fast as they can,
keeping the world abuzz with
wings and bodies in droves in rain.

SUNDAY CHILDREN

I remember most clearly
one child, barefoot,
carrying a naked infant
in a travelling cloth.

I followed them up the aisle,
nearly tripping over her
as she fell to genuflect
with the infant on her hip;

she almost dropped him,
head flopping over
the crook in her elbow,
as she made the sign of the cross.

GOSPEL & OFFERTORY

There's dancing during the procession
and dancing in the offertory; the offerings
are avocados, a live chicken, matoke
bananas, mangoes, beans, sometimes shillings,
even a young bull at Raphael's ordination Mass.
There's no passing the basket;
we walk to the altar in random order
to present our offerings. Once, sitting
by the choir, I saw a woman make change
from the basket for her thousand shillings.
Others watched her brush the mangoes aside
looking for a five hundred coin, no one cared.
She proves me surprised by joy at the
private made public; glory to God, lord of the dance.

BACKLESS PEWS

Slat seats upon slat legs upon
two-by-fours parallel to the aisle
under slat kneelers, the pews held us—
short and dark and crop-haired (all
except Christine and me)—for Masses
and weddings and baptisms and

women's meetings. Sundays on the backless
pews we sat hunched from endless homilies.
We sat so long at Raphael's ordination Mass
I felt my bones would push through
my flesh and I would seep from two
round holes through my dress.

I watched a boy slump and hunch until
his grandfather slipped an arm behind to catch him,
tilt him into his chest. I watched a girl
go outside to climb for *paw-paw* while
Father Paul droned on and on in Luganda.
I watched a leaf-wrapped chicken

roll, unbalanced from left to right under the
backless pews. I watched Gerald
watch his mother fray the ends of her
gomesi sleeves, separate the blue and white
threads and weave them, slat upon slat,
into thick and thin stripes, like backless pews.

WEDNESDAY MORNING CHARISMA

Crowding the plank altar,
      six drummers in a u-shape,
women-mothers, women-farmers,
traveling cloths spread on the ground,
      eyes in a reverie and babies crawling
          between the close drums.
Gerald and I just to the side, where the choir would be.
      Without a word you scoop a baby,
    she's on your lap, leaning into your chest;
        when we kneel she's suspended in your arms.
Muzeyi in gumboots raises her hands out
      palms down, kneeling, chanting, singing

Ayi Mukama, otenderezawe, otenderezawe, otenderezawe, Ayi Mukama

Crawling to his mother, a baby unbuttons her *gomesi*,
      nurses while she's drumming.
Her hands beat and beat as Muzeyi changes to a responsorial
    three beat variation
        naruhanga,
      and three and a half beats
      naruhanga.
It's dense, the room, the drums, the words, the melody
      up and down, packed into space
        if sound can pack.
I'm lost, staring at the child in your lap,
      following your lead,
       sitting, kneeling, standing,

sitting, kneeling,
no clue of the words until

O God, you whisper, O God I glorify you,
O Lord, I praise you, I am created for you.
O God, I pray, O God I'm intruding,
O Lord, is this my faith, I am wandering and overtaken.

RAPHAEL'S PRAYER IN KYAKATEBE

But I try, Lord, to follow this calling;
I look from behind the chicken coop
to the parishioners gathered
before my parent's matoke plantation
and see the women standing with their
wailing babies and the other priests passing
through them with oil and water and a basin.
I don't know a holier sight than these women—
this woman in the dark green *gomesi*
with her child still pink just four days old,
this proud woman in the peach *gomesi*
with her fat child; she is singing out and
not taking notice as he unbuttons to nurse.
Though I walk amongst them with
my vial of water and oil, I'll never know
what springs feed them or how
love grows as it divides.

PROVERB VII: THE CHICKEN

When the chicken drinks water,
it lifts its head to heaven.
Even the chicken prays.
There's a chicken in the basket
this Sunday. Put there by a
girl, no older than my first memories
of myself. She came forward with
the bird wrapped in banana
leaves and tied with the strong
fibers that come from the center
of each leaf. When she approached
the altar, she paused, her feet
touching on the inside surfaces,
ankles pressed together, and bent
to the low brick to place the chicken
in the basket. It looked at her
and clucked from the basket,
raising its feather head to the altar.
She turned and left, back to her bench—
eyes closed, knees knocking together,
even the palms of her hands still pressing.

PAIR II: THE FIREFLY

I always thought of fireflies as joyous,
glowing green in the grass. But tonight
one crawled up the wall in our room.
It walked aimlessly, left and right,
lighting every 5 or 7 seconds.
I could see the whole body; it was
a different creature than when dozens
gather and a light is always lit.

In Luganda, the Alleluia and *Amena*
make me forget about malaria and AIDS,
well water and rape, hunger and pocked blackboards.
I wonder if Nandugwa ever forgets—
kneeling is requisite and coffins are
made of short boards, so short they seem
to be made of spares. Spares are
grouped for sale on the side of the road,
the tops resting skewed until later.

Nandugwa must have walked amongst
the spares, lifting each top to see the
wood inside. Lifting and setting,
lifting the light board, the light of
fireflies, in groups lighting and lifting
at dusk in the churchyard far from the road.

BEES

Dry season setting in, cows' bones showing through,
my brothers and I are home from school for lunch,
but the coop is full of feathers and bones, not eggs.

Paw-paw falling and the *pichi-pichi* coming louder,
Matthias and Paschal and I pick fallen fruit,
paw-paw and jackfruit and passion fruit, avocados;

the goats pulled loose from the cassava tree and
ate the roots. I climb up for jackfruit and toss it
down at Matthias. Climbing out the branch,

I lie on my stomach, wrap my arms around the
branch and watch as Paschal finds a beehive again,
across the path under the low branches of the passion fruit.

He takes a stick to prod around; Matthias joins
to stir loose the murmurous haunt.
Paschal and Matthias run to the coop, the bees

don't see me but they see the goats tied to the
passionfruit tree and I hold the branch tighter with
my knees, tuck my feet up so the sole of one cups

the top of the other, the goats wail like drunks
by the butcher's shop; lumps cover their hides,
Taata jumps off his bike and beats the goats with his shirt.

TAXI CONDUCTOR & DRIVER

We were over capacity to begin with,
seventeen passengers, *Ssebo!* We'd
never pass the military checkpoints.
I didn't know why you were pulling over
for more passengers, until I looked
to the side of the road and saw a
white woman, red dress, and a black man
beside her. But where do we put her?
The man led her to the backbench;
they must be going to Kampala.
She's hunched up so the back
of her neck is touching on the metal
roof of the taxi, hair hanging
like strings of frayed hog rope.
There isn't enough room,
why can't we put her up front with us?
Why won't she leave him? He pulls a child,
purple dress, from the bench to his lap,
and the *muzungu* slips next to him,
slides her arm between his arm and the child's.
We're jumping forward, jolting along,
weaving to miss the bigger potholes;
soon the child sleeps, leaning forward
over the man's arms and the white woman
sleeps against his shoulder and he
sleeps against the back of the child.

PROVERB VIII: A STRAWBERRY BLOSSOM

A strawberry blossom
will not moisten dry bread.
How could I have known
the dimensions of a child's coffin
the carpenter's unsteady hands
fitting the dovetails and pegging
the top shut. How many family graves
will I know, scattered at the edges
of our farmland? How many never-breaking
fevers will I try to excise, my
daughter's death and my
husband's suicide; hanging
one-legged from the jackfruit tree.
How many moaning nights?
We're burying her and digging a pit
for him and cutting the rope.
How many buried swaddling cloths?
At the end, blood drooled from the corners
of her young mouth, her lids
stayed open as her eyes went slack.
How could I have known?

TURNING UGANDAN

I.
It's late. I'm finally getting a chance to bathe.
Ten o'clock, we've had darkness for three hours.
I light the white taper, mix hot water with the rain,
set the basin on the low stool, hang my face over the steam,
let my mind calm, shut my eyes, begin this ritual.

Soak the rag, rub it with soap, squeeze it over my
salty body; soak my hair, rub it with soap,
squeeze water on my head, God I'm slow tonight.
Sing—Bind us Together, Lord—and wash my feet.
They're black. My hands are black. My arms
are black. I continue washing. Standing up,
I see my white stomach and frown.

II.
You brought Boombikale with a fever of 41,
we tried panadol syrup but the fussy boy wouldn't swallow.
You pinched his cheeks to open his lips. He coughed,
the five sticky milliliters erupted up onto my glasses,
my face, your face, your hands. I wet a rag, wiped
your hands and face, and met your eyes close to my own
as I knelt before you. You averted them, even Boombikale
stopped crying and twisted away. *Sitti cawoo; sitti cawoo sitti cawoo.*

III.
In the crowded taxi licensed for fourteen passengers
we are twenty-six with five on this back bench
and four sacks of matoke under us. I'm sweating
through my dress and can't keep my head up—

neither can you. You might be twenty,
leaning on me, asleep. My head down,
I look at you—your trousers have holes
in the side seams, your feet are bare, your body
smells but it smells like mine; I rest against you,
your head anchoring my shoulder and I smile
the man to my left has folded his newspaper,
leans his head on my shoulder and I am another—
smelly, cramped, exhausted, anonymous.

ANTENATAL CLINIC

Woman after woman, we witness through our hands.
Measure the finger widths from pelvic bone to naval,
subtract the finger widths from naval to the top
of her belly. Three. 33 weeks along.

Place my hands on both sides of her belly
feel for the head, press, close my eyes.
The baby lies crosswise, head facing left.
From the head, I sense where the heart is,

press my ear to the fetal scope, hold my hands out,
like the priest's cupped hovering hands
over the host just before it becomes the Body.
The heartbeat is faint, I listen closely,

press my ear harder, the beat is steady,
my tears are dripping onto this woman's belly,
rolling down like salty wet lines of longitude,
she from one side and me from the other

of this sphere; she is everything, only for a moment;
her daughter and her daughter's daughter will
keep burying their children and their sister's children
and their husbands will marry and marry.

Press my hand to her baby's head, with my other hand
I hold the woman's neck as she comes to sitting.
I follow the baby's head downward to the pelvis.
With our three heads near to touching, I remember

the dusk through the mango tree leaves, the gray lace shapes,
the black shadows they make. I know we also
make shapes and dusk comes through us.

IMMUNIZING IN BUKOBA

I.
Ninety-four women gathered with their babies
on 11 June 2003 in the village of Bukoba
in Mubende district for polio, tetanus, tuberculosis,
diphtheria, hepatitis B, and whooping cough vaccinations.

There was a woman with a pale green scarf
tied around her shaved head, waiting on the first bench.
When her baby started to pee, she set it on the dirt floor
between her feet. When he was done, she picked him up
and opened her *gomesi* to nurse him on cracked nipples.

II.
We laid the needles and pills out at a school,
sent the teacher and his students in
thin blue shirts and dresses home for the day
so we could use their space to weigh babies and vaccinate.
The girls fourteen and older stayed because
they are childbearing age and need tetanus vaccines.

The woman, 17, whose second child, 3 months old,
weighed just under 4 kilos and drooled down my dress
as I bent over to place him in the suspended shorts
for weighing, was later bent over her son, singing
in Luganda and restraining him during the tetanus shot.

III.
The roof of the schoolhouse had holes in the thatching
to let light in. The brickwork was crumbling

and children tumbled around the holes
to see their first glimpse of *Bazungu*.

The woman with the pale yellow *gomesi*, Naalongo,
with twin girls, 11 months old, didn't know their birth date,
their birth weight, or the spelling of her name.
They walked from Kyiya at dawn and left Bukoba at 7.

IV.
The blackboards were pieced from bits,
the dirt floors swept bare. There were
no desks and the benches splintered and bowed.

The woman with a short neck and broad nose curving
toward her lips handed her screaming son to me
for weighing; as he caught sight of my face
he stopped crying and reached his hands to my glasses.

V.
Outside the schoolhouse, a game of soccer was
going on; barefoot with a ball of rags,
children chased through the oncoming dusk
like raindrops dancing on a cowhide drum.

There was a woman, thirty years old, who had
lost three children to AIDS and brought her infant
for vaccination. Her husband saw a prostitute
and brought back the promise of her early grave
after eight months of marriage. Her lips

are the only full part of her left and they are thick,
fading into her mouth a deep menstrual red.

VI.
I crouched over the pit latrine at midday,
the sun radiating through the thatching
just above my head. Standing up, I nearly
knocked the low cover over; I made myself
a shunt to the roof as I let my skirt back down.

A broad-shouldered woman, Proscovia, twenty years old,
brought her son, Kevina Kawgu, two months old.
His belly button was protruding three centimeters
and there was a ring of raw skin around his neck
and sores in his mouth. His eyeballs were distended
(though not as much as his mother's) and he had
lesions on his eyelids. His tonsils were white and
swollen and his arms were covered in scabs.

VII.
Through the crowd, Joyce the midwife weaves a way
from woman to woman to give iron tablets
and listen for heartbeats and tell the young women
to push when it comes time. Joyce lost six grown children
to AIDS and now cares for her grandkids; she tells
one woman to pray for twins and eat more avocados.

Nakalanzi Lucia's son, Luke Ndayambazi, was three months old.
They walked from Kawci. She knows her other children
have syphilis and now Luke's bald scalp is covered in sores
and he won't nurse. The injections are five hundred shillings each.

IX.
Under the coming moon, a woman grabbed her
infant by the wrist and swung him around
her body to her back as she hunched forward
and tied the traveling cloth around first over her
breasts and then around her waist. Standing up
she reached behind to shift him into place.

There was a pregnant woman who looked bigger
than the rest; Sister Pascazia predicted twins.
The woman's face opened wide and as she turned
looking over her shoulder, reveling a neck of
tendons and skin so tight that the lines of her
throat cartilage showed under her jaw.

I THOUGHT SHE WAS SINGING

I looked out the window, I thought
she was singing. Three women,
one large in the middle, two thin
on the sides, nearly to the edge

of the dispensary land, and the
middle woman sank to a deep squat.
One baby tore out with its large head;
she was ashen, armless, still.

The women sang, lowering the mother
fully to the ground, laying her back
on the grass, and curling her knees
onto her belly. A smaller baby pushed

against her bones; out of nowhere
her legs shot up, soles to sky.
Our midwife pushed her hand
into the woman as the child tried to slip

cord first into the world. She pushed
the baby into the mother and slid the cord
in front of her face, down her tiny body.
How did she pull her hand out again

and quickly catch this small twin
swimming out face down? The midwife
wrapped her pink body in the mother's
travelling cloth like ears of roasted maize.

Oh—their singing—from the body,
of the body—is not simple.
The large, full song is the body is
wailing and singing—those who have not

known the extremes of both pains
can never understand the difference.
I looked out the window at
four women, two infants, one placenta

aching out right here, right between
the dispensary and convent.
Those who know extremes, can never
fully love those of us who are ignorant.

I GIVE THANKS FOR EXCESSES

For a margin around this paper,
for black ink and blue.

For vegetable peelers and pots with handles,
for children without AIDS.

Joyce, the midwife, has been giving thanks
for years. Into her forties now,

she claims to hate a first time mother:
"she just opens her mouth and screams.

I want to tell her to clamp her mouth and push!"
She tells me it's better when she's

already had kids, she knows what to do,
when to rest, when the head is near

and can push it into my palm. Six of her own nine
have died of AIDS in adulthood.

Some tell you it gets easier, the more children you have,
but it doesn't, she tells me, you just learn

to hurt and get the baby out faster. It doesn't
get easier, you can't escape AIDS,

you're either infected or affected. I give thanks
for the excess of years I will have

for the chance to not give birth, for the
ink to write, the margins to hold me.

THE ARTIST, THE ART

I. *Scale Boy, Kampala*

I stepped off the curb and arched back,
avoiding a bicycle carrying two foot-tied chickens.
Again I started across and arched back
for a *boda-boda* with a mother and baby.
Finally I crossed, and one scale boy
crouched with feet up by his hips
and knees pressed together. He fingered
the smooth edge of his scale, the raised
rubber foot pad, and pressed his eyes shut
as he traced the shape of the scale's feet
and then his own feet. He kept his eyes shut
as I walked past, from the east taxi park to the west.

II. *The Artist*

How do I justify the artist? I'm so far
from the words of suffering that they've
become colloquial: slum, ghetto, thin,
sick, starving. Does the scale boy know
that his starving face makes his eyes so big
they glisten with beauty and makes his
hip bones stick out like tails of fish, blunt
above his drooping trousers; the heads of the fish
are the two bony clusters above either side
of his tailbone. How do I justify the artist?

Sometimes I don't wash my hair, sometimes
I watch and mimic a sooty chat with my
shoulders hunched around my ears and my chin
tucked into my chest with what I'd like to think
might be humility. As if all this wasn't also art
or play at beauty. As if it gets me farther from myself.

III. *Kiganda Parish Rosary Maker*

He sat cross-legged on a mat in front of the office
Father Paul shared with Father Peter. His thick
thumbnails curved the wire around each
several-sided blue or white or green bead.
Six finished rosaries lay in front of his knees;
they showed his tightness with wire, his frugality.
Rolled pant legs revealed a ring of old sores
around his ankles. This silent man turned
his yellowed eyes to me and smiled, toothless.
If you're thinking it was a carefree smile
of a simple, holy man, it wasn't. In his lips,
caved around his gums, in his cloudy eyes,
was an intimacy that shook me—you are
living and dying with us, in the same world,
at the same time, whether you see us or not.

IV. *This is the Body*

This is the body, crouched next to a scale
to sell the service of weighing yourself. This
is the body, letting its hair grow dirty and limp—
false poverty. This is the body, making rosaries
and sitting for hours. This is the body,
contorted in pain from AIDS—or syphilis—
or malaria—or diarrhea—this is the human body.

III.

CONSTANT

WASHING DAY WITH GERALD

Stilted glances and touches
become play and sport with our labor—
soak, scrub, rinse, scrub, rinse.

Neighbors stop with jugs on their heads
on their way to the well when they see
this white woman in the village,

scrubbing clothes and sheets.
The Blessed Mary and all her beads
come out from under your shirt

and the backs of my arms turn pink with the sun,
the sweat pours down from your hairline
and the water turns red brown like the earth.

The coarse linen wills us to softness
and the soft soap melts me to prayer—
that the passion fruit grow riper
and the laundry take longer
for ever and ever amen.

WALKING TO THE WELL

Stumbling on the path between the jackfruit trees
and the rocks, knocking her empty yellow jug
against her heels as it bounced along behind her,
her brother close on her right carried another
jug and they followed us at a distance.

I stopped to take their jugs and you stopped
to take their hands and the little trinity followed me
up towards the well, you towering between them.
When our paths parted, the brother pried
his sister's hand from yours, one finger at a time.

The next day, walking dark and light in the dusk
down Mpologoma Hill, you took the full jug from the girl,
silently carried it with one hand to her house.
Catching my gaze, you pause
and chide, "shush, you are entering me."

I admit I try; but it's you—my eucharistic
minister on Sundays, my seventy-one extra kilos
at night—coming through me. When the
girl won't leave your hand, it's me who won't
let go of her jug. You take her to the well and carry
more than she could. Your white teeth grit in strain.

SCYTHE SINGER

Swing and drop, arc and swing,
the drop of each side catches me most—
or the pause and drop—or the pause,
step, and drop. Or the one movement—
not the distinct parts. Gerald scythes
the convent yard on Tuesday mornings
after Mass—really it's the job of the
boys who stay with the nuns for school—
but they tire so Gerald leaves his shirt
on the rail, takes off his belt to
roll the waist of his pants, even
leaves his shoes at this collection
and he looks like a boy—making the
scythe sing like breath through
clenched teeth and illuminating bare skin
with sweat in the morning heat
in front of the convent.

THE LUGANDA LESSON

The first night, stretched across the mat, talking of the seminary
with Arlene, Gerald smelled of sleep, and I let my mind go—
what would that body look like stretched out in bed?

Up the hill at the *tonto* spot, Mary is asleep in my arms,
dreaming herself home to the home she misses; your dreams
go home, I know, because in the morning I saw my pink shirt,

Ndikwambala nga ekooti
I wear you like a watch

draped across your pillow with an impression of your head.
I didn't ask for it back, hoping you might want it and use it,
and later me. Putting it on, I smell beans and fallen jackfruit.

As you drum on my back, I learn Luganda slowly,
hearing you through my ear to your bony chest.
When I raise myself—a cobra—you stop singing

Ndikwambala nga essaawa
I wear you like a coat

until I lie down. Mmmm, you say, the most important part.
Try *Oli otya. Mmm. Bilungi. Mmm. Oli otya. Mmm.* Sustain the
        sound,
mmm fills us—a note held by the bass of the choir.

Not saying *mmm* means you'll listen but you don't want to.
Your letter came today. "Dear Swettie," I laugh,

"thank you for the pictures. I want to make flames for them."
Kubanga nze nkwagala nnyo siri kusuula lilah
I will never lose you

In Luganda, *l* and *r* interchange. I knew *mmm* would fade,
I knew my shirt would smell like cheap detergent again,
but I'm still learning Luganda, I'm checking out books, so

please don't make flames just hold your bass note longer *omwana*
I've learned there is no genitive in Luganda, *bambi owange.*

CHEWING

I.

In the beginning, the meat was tender,
flavored with chili powder, salt; as the
weeks passed, the meat grew tough;
chewing, I would finds bits of
bone and gristle. "Take more hard meat,"
you said at lunch, "always take more,
always more to be taken."

II.

On the back of the motorcycle, sidesaddle
as you drove to market, you asked,
"are you secure?" and the word came out
se-chewer. Yes, hooking my fingers
around your hip bones, thumbs through
your belt, twisting my torso so my breasts
leaned square into your shoulder blades,
I was ready when the bike climbed gears.

III.

Before cooking the dinner beef,
a cutting from the same old cow,
you kneaded coarse salt, pushing
into its rawness with the palms
of your hands, trying to soften
its fibers. Trying to keep me
from looking at your bleeding hand
you asked, "I'm curious, how is Fildah?"
and the word came out chew-rious.

IV.
Your hand bled into the meat,
the meat bled into the wooden board,
and after dinner, while everyone slept,
we continued chewing. The vestiges
of your salty palm blood pressed into
my temples as we sang psalms
in the farthest garden. You claimed
you could hear me through your hands,
so I sang in my body through your palms.

GERALD OF KIGANDA

Smiling with that odd dimple after four and a half hours
of Raphael's deaconate Mass with seventy-four baptisms,

"you must be tired." No, but I know my brows are furrowing.
You're wearing a white cassock with cloth-covered buttons.

The white shawl makes a clamshell of your shoulders.
I wonder who pressed it this morning, it wasn't me;

there isn't one charcoal smudge. I fall into that pursed look
because you're not perfect, heaven help your cooks

if you ever do become a priest and heaven help me
if you don't. You're mortal, forged in the pot of transgressions,

but holy, holy Lord, twelfth of thirteen, you're young.
Born too late for your father's canings but in time for him
to take you to his carpentry shop and teach you to bevel this world.

CONSTANT

When I walk from the house to the latrine,
I am stopped in the dark when I look up.

I look up with purpose night after night
because the stars are packed tightly

like the children crowded on the bench
by *muzeyi* at Mass. They don't notice

that there isn't enough room on the kneelers
after communion, they just tumble and fold

capriciously on top of one another.
When I come back in and pump the steamer

you help me light the *waragi* and I am stopped again
when I see our skin, forearm to forearm,

palm over fist as I try again: how rich the sky is,
how bright this star, how dark, how heavenly dark

you are. You who like everything thickly concentrated
like your stars, your fellow parishioners: local brew,

salt on your pork, ginger in your coffee, egg yolks,
and sugar in the passion fruit juice.

BETRAYALS

What language will our children speak?
A question you asked me twice.
First, I was bathing behind the latrine,
cupping and pouring rainwater,
watching the candlelight in the basin.
You stood on the other side, shucking maize.

I heard you tell your Mother hello—
hi, hi—it's American English for
'How are you.' Ah—now I understand
your response when I greeted you
outside the dispensary, my fingers
dusty with mefloquine—"hi," I said.
"Fine," you replied, "how are you?"

Weeks later, you asked me a second time
as we walked the muddy path
from school to home for lunch.
Rain beaded on your bare neck.
Perhaps I should have corrected you,
explained the proper response to hello,
but it seemed our only lack in communication

was its excess. Our children have dipped
themselves in black ink. They traipse
naked, slapping their feet on the paths
toward the pineapple grove,
the hen house, the grazing field.
Forgive them, Gerald. They speak
in tongues to you. So heavy with our

creation, their English is too much my own.
The weight of your folly, your leaning
toward my dustiness, your assuredness
that is lost when you know your funny grammar,
pressed into the fibers of your sleeves,
like the mefloquine I rubbed there. What
language will our children speak? The water
in the basin ripples my reply, my excess.
Chill water in the night, swathe us, look on.

DARK UNDER KIGANDA STARS

Dark under Kiganda stars, the night dove was calling
when Arlene came home feverish with the flu.
That was the night you rubbed antiseptic balm
to coat the inside of my nose and ears and she put
ginger in her porridge and chewed the pork bones after dinner.
Dark under Kiganda stars, the night dove was calling
when I pressed your pink shirt and burned my arm
swinging the charcoal iron to heat it up again.
That was the night I discovered endearments
in English directly translated from Luganda—
I was a lion with hair of molten lava.
Dark under Kiganda stars, the night dove was calling
and I saw your eyes open slowly after sleeping
with the rhythm of a slow procession drum;
that was the night they also opened quickly,
like a startled chicken beating its wings
from chest to sky, when I kicked the tin of shoe polish.
Dark under Kiganda stars, the night dove was calling
when your eyes didn't blink and, pink tongue between
white teeth between brown lips, you whispered, "I'm so black."
That was the night you tried to remember
the passage from Kunitz's "King of the River"
I did not choose the way, the way chose me.
Dark under Kiganda stars, the night dove was calling
when you stumbled and asked me to practice
Luganda—*Nkwagala. Sula bulungi*
That was the night we listened to the rain make mud.

WHEN GERALD BEATS THE BEAN PODS

When Gerald beats the bean pods
out behind the house, his skin
grows blacker in the highest sun.

Come, Gerald, with your bean-beating pole,
come and swing it around your back,
down to the beans raked out on the ground.

When Gerald beats the bean pods
and the chickens scatter, his eyes
grow hot and salt-bleary.

Come, Gerald, to the jug of well water.
Muddled and unboiled, warm like breath,
don't spill a drop to bead on the dust.

When Gerald beats the bean pods
the pole grows heavy, pulling long
his triceps as he reaches the back swing.

Come, Gerald, shining tree, no aching eyes,
no callused, heated palms, no spare, dried, and curled
bean pods found days later uneaten by the cow

will escape the coming fevers for you—
now I—and ours. Life will thin and fail.
Slow your swing now, speed it when we

grow blacker in the highest stages. When
the heat fades and the rain slows,
slip edgewise down the bean path.

EVERY TIME

But we're not taken over every time;
or any time; we're calculated.
We're fitting this hand to that one
beneath the cover of my coarse
canvas bag. We're slowly working
this eye to that one and you
turn away. We're not even overtaken
alone; we're folding this leg round
that, quietly, the rag mattress
and plank bed swear not to give us
away. We're not overtaken in
this space upon which we're imprinted,
like Keats' lovers chasing on the urn,
you leave first in the mornings
and I greet you, as if for the first time,
by the charcoal stove and we
boil eggs. We never embraced nor
ever parted, we stood ever hopeful
and privately watchful, painted
onto this earthly matter.
In league together, or I in league
with you, there was one overtaking:
in grief, not knowing how to keep
our painted features, you embraced me
and fell to the concrete floor of your room.
I sank with you and, the room, the light,
the space around us became a shell—
in my mind, that is the every time, the overtaking.

TWENGE, TU'ZI, GULU

The light brown cow
    Bilungi
        licked the shoulder
of the dark brown cow
    this morning.
Her tongue was pale
    as a thick fish's tail
        soft over the bony shoulder
she can't caress
    any other way,
        can't speak words to,
and so it is for us;
    now when you ask
"can I feel your warmth?"
    all I say is yes.
My words are dry,
there is nothing else
    to give.
        Love came
        too quickly, dear,
now we're goose-stepping
    over windfall mangoes
        but things are fine
if I lick your shoulders,
    bloom in the night
    with the heliotrope;
        things are fine
with a little wine, drops of water, and heaven.

TO COMFORT

It seems to work: when a baby cries,
the mom lays it belly down across her
thighs and cups the upper curve of its bottom.

She works her hands back and forth
in a fast pace that could never calm a child—
but does. Her hands aren't rubbing, aren't stroking

the skin, just holding the skin in place
while the hands move. When I crumpled
at the side of the bed in tears over

this syphilitic child today at the dispensary,
you didn't hold me, you didn't talk;
you lifted me to the length of your body,

let me lie there as you cupped your hands
on the curve of each shoulder blade and
rocked me. It didn't work.

But I tried it at the dispensary,
tried to work a baby into calm,
a baby crying with me as her mom

was weighed and examined. I started to do
this little rocking, and realized it wasn't
the baby calmed first, it was me.

The baby exhaled in gusts and I felt
her neck muscles relax into my thighs;
her hands worked open like a waxbill dipping

and unwrapping its feet from a snag.
The next time you rocked me, I stopped
thinking, word obsessing.

All the layers of dross gone, all but the fire
of warmth and heart-stopping work, and now
belly down, it seems to work.

PROVERB IX: FOREWARNED, FOREARMED

The one I never understood—
the one I share and try but can't
understand in language, only in
a physical sense. Forewarned,

forearmed. You first said it,
palm on the back of my neck
as I stooped to the charcoal stove
to roast maize. "Don't burn yourself."

As I ironed my paneled linen skirt
and swung the heavy charcoal box
in slow arcs to heat it back up,
"Don't burn yourself," you said.

As I walked to school,
"don't burn yourself, take my
long shirt." Forewarned,
forearmed. When a proverb

seems thin, is there thickness
at all in the world? If I
iron just so, or walk
just so, or crouch just so

by the stove, my sweat dripping
all over Kiganda, will I ever
forewarn myself—or forearm
myself—or forgive my failure?

FRIED TALIPAH IN GGABA

Plunging your hooked little finger in the fish's eye socket, you
        scoop around,
pull out the gel covering the hard pit of the eyeball, and slip it into
        your mouth.

I don't know why you do this, and yet I expect it and play along. I
        know you want me
to look, to cringe, and take another bite of white flesh to rid my
        mouth of the phantom texture

of eye socket fluids. So I do. When you teach me a new phrase in
        Luganda and
wait for me to try it and you laugh and say it again, I know I fail.
        I'll never eat

the fish's eye gel, but when I put on a *gomesi* for the first time, you
        were
surprised by my comfort; even with my skin I could wear the
        darkest gold.

What have you done but fished me out? I'll never be a Baganda,
        I'll never pronounce
the *ng* correctly, I'll always forget to kneel sometimes, and I can't
        even promise

to understand all the parts of Mass here. But I'll never be rid of
        the sounds of your
language, especially the choir of St. Mugaga and their drums; I see
        men greet each other

here with a slap on the back or a punch to the arm and think of
        you, greeting Migadde Vicent
"Eh, Ssebo" full in the throat but coming out soft with a touch and
        a touch of foreheads.

I'll never forget walking through Nakiganda Market past the
        butcher's stand with his quarter
cow and leg of pig and live chicken hanging from the crossbeam of
        the stand. He stopped

mid-chop with his cleaver in the air and jaw down almost to the
        dip in his collarbone
before plunging on for the customer. I'll never forget being late to
        school because I

was swarmed in the trading center after I took the hand of one
child and the rest came out from their peeking places to hold all
along the length of my arm and play with my loose elbow skin.

I still don't have anything resolved, why you show me our
        differences—eye gel and language,
gomesi and greetings, taxis and butchers and skin—and you revel
        in my cringing, my

botched Luganda, my equally dropped jaw at the butcher. I am
        tired and ready
to cook in pots with handles and have ice, but that's not culture
        and I don't know

what is. I'm losing it. I eat fried fish, wear a *gomesi*, and some
        times even forget that I'm white
but you never do, and that desiccates me; I can't leave this dress,
        this butcher, these children

and I certainly can't bring them home. I am so thirsty, so dry for
        tonto so I hook
my little finger and put it in the eye socket because I just want to
        eat the eye gel.

I WOKE THIS MORNING

I woke this morning to find your head on my belly—
on my right side, resting where my thigh becomes my stomach.
Your arms were wrapped around my thigh, your knees
were bent on either side of my foot, and your eyes were closed.
I could feel your breath on my thigh and the intake that expanded
      your chest.

The rooster was crowing—it had been since five—and the narrow
                cow
was standing just outside our window, calling out for you to wake.
Sometime in the night a fly drowned in our glass of tonto. You
      looked solid.
I was surprised when you spoke, "I'm going to start tea,
the sun is up." How did you know I was awake?

You told me my quadriceps tightened around you and when you
flexed your biceps around my thigh, (I hadn't noticed) I flexed
my thigh in response. How strange, what I tell you before I know
I'm awake. How strange, the details you notice, how strange
that I'm never awake first, how awful and strange.

SLOUGH STRAY

Gerald claimed it was the case once,
that a stray came to him from the slough.
He pulled her face to his own: the damp
breath of the dog warmed his sloping,
spreading nose. He cast his eyes down,
remembering the dog's tail pulled tight
to its belly; he stayed low until each fair lamp—
soles and kneebacks, hip flesh and elbow crooks,
cheek hollows, even the edges of his
receding curls—each lamp was lit
with oil and heat from my own nose.
Is this vulgar? Me, on my hands and knees
above him; he, a tail to my belly; me, anticipating
the lamps toppling and catching fire to the hay
beneath us. It was beneath the slough stray,
even in our passion it was burning.

PROVERB X: THE LAME HORSE

When the horse goes lame
it kicks and kicks and is still
happy. Even the lame horse
is happy in its own way.

Sometimes in the mornings
you'd sing to yourself,
Ndkwambala nga ekooti
and all the other phrases

I can't remember, but you'd
begin before rising, before
waking, almost before
breathing, it seemed.

I can't understand it, can't
replicate the melody, but
it's so much a part of my
own breathing and waking

that the mornings you don't
sing, I miss my lameness
of not knowing, I miss being
other, I suppose. It was the

mornings of your singing that
I was most other, most lame.
When we rose silent
to the morning work and went

out kicking together, were we
both lame horses? Did I
still share the odors, the quiet,
did I breathe your silence?

OF MAGDALENE

I.
I asked you to write the address
of the seminary. Your name in
scrolling penmanship, Gerald Lilah,
crossed the page; you said simply,
"This is our name, can't I use it?"
But there are rules for naming.
The paternal grandfather names a child.
Twins girls are Babirye and Nakato,
twin boys are Wasswa and Kato.
The mother of twins is Nnaalongo,
the father of twins is Ssaalongo.

II.
Erinya lyo gwe 'ani you say
kneeling in the back room
on the dusty floor, cassava flour storage
behind you, your knees butted up
against my bare toes. I didn't understand
the significance of a man kneeling.
My sin was too much haste and hope.

III.
You chose for me my only saint's name,
Magdalene, you searched the book
with tenderness and Father Joseph blessed
me. You're naming yourself now,
with me. Lilah isn't a saint's name, you can keep
Gerald's feast day, put my name your pocket
like your handkerchief; it's supplementary.

I'll sign our name on my letters, Lilah Gerald.
On your improbable passport, the embassy
can stamp their unlikely visa over your name,
Gerald Lilah. We'll be a circle.
I'll flank you in my letters, in your passport,
as you travel on the inside from *boda* to *boda*.

GERALD'S PRAYER IN GULU

Mother Mary, it was you who taught
us to call on you as mother. I'm so
far from mine now so I call on you.
My own mother would take the small
ones—me, Matthias, and Arlene—to her
bed when we were young and Amin's soldiers
prowled our village; my own mother
would cover my ears, one with her hand
and one with her chest as she rocked
me and sometimes left the bed to cower
under the window; my own mother
would pray for me and keep me safe
all the days of my youth. I am gone now
but not a man; Mary pray for me, rock me,
cover my ears, fold me to your own dark chest.

GERALD: SLEEPING MOST NIGHTS
UNDER MY BED

I was alone for the first time and far north from my home.
I was away, praying: six in the morning, noon, five in the evening.

On my second night in Gulu, I was studying Hebrew and near to
    sleep
when Kony rebels waited by the water tank between the dorm

and chapel. The headmaster woke us much later from the thick of
    night
he was a shaking banana leaf pelted with rain, he was quiet, he
    shifted

from room to room, bed to bed shaking us from our beds
to the cool concrete under the metal frames. Four seminarians,

first year boys like me, had gone for washing later than the rest.
They were stabbed behind the water tank and our headmaster
    found them

skewered to the ground. We didn't sleep that night. On the second
    Monday,
I bathed at nine and prayed. I gathered the lantern close to the iron
    bedpost

and pulled my blanket to the floor with me. I turned down the
    lantern
almost immediately to lie in the dark and listen to the gunshots and

the villagers as they tucked their children into the wooden pews
and themselves into grass beds close to the dormitory walls.

On the third Monday, I flipped my bed to stand on the tops of its
      head posts
and foot posts and with the extra inches, I would lie under it most
      evenings

with the lantern on, still reading, still writing feverishly about
Hagar and Sarah, Esther and Judith, and later the twelve, the four,
      the One.

MORNINGS WITH THE CALF

The cow starts her lowing early,
so early in these 12-hour balanced days

that the sun is still half down, half
waiting, letting that voice carry itself

north like the Nile currents. Decanting her
long moan, letting it come through the

ventilating bricks and open doorways
she's near. Her calf is dying, its jowls fill

heavy with fluid; the capillaries
leak and blood comes through

the short fur between the two small columns
of her jawbones. Mornings I still greet

the calf lying under the mango tree,
kneel to her shadow head and stroke

the sides of her face. I still reach my hands
to the wet underside of her throat,

and follow the stubble fur from chin to chest
in slow arcs. My hands come up ruddy brown

with earth and blood and I stroke her again,
resting my ear to her flat nose top.

I still join in her tidal breathing, the thick
in and out of the ever, the ever after.

PROVERB XI: THE WHITENESS OF MY TEETH

It is the whiteness of my teeth
that troubles me, you say.
There is no way to excise
the pain from your chest
the night before my departure.
I learn to apologize, ask
forgiveness; you soften
your shoulders away from
your ears and press your
palms to the crown of my head.
Anointing oil of your thick-veined
hands, let me shut my eyes and
chew my bottom lip, revealing
a bit of tooth and blood. It is
to show the whiteness
of our teeth that we laugh.

BLACKER

Kiganda was, to me, a chaos
at first. Black would shine
to orange and I would seep

my tea orange to black
as the sun rose with the
cock, cow, calf. I never noticed

the order until I began to number
the days. You seeped those mornings,
from black to blacker. I knew

your color was sleep's trick when
I began to remember our days.
Truly, you seeped from orange,

that deep melon I could not know,
to black, to blacker, to a sheen of ink.
I pretended once that your face

became so black it turned from
chocolate to tea to a moonless, starless
chaos: sky. Ordinary vision, seeping.

LAYERS

Red, auburn, brown, peat, wood chip, dirt.
Every human color; Gerald's skin
at the base of it all. Mid-November,

the rainy season finally claimed the calf.
This morning, Gerald wrote, a honeyguide
blinked her wings, dropped rain
beneath my unpruned banana leaves.
She flew low, skidded under the trough,

died: orange, yellow, black, water, dirt,
buried white matoke peelings. Our skin
is underground where the cow stands.
I've stopped sleeping in my bed. Last night
I stayed with Nala-dog by the kitchen:

space, stars, black sky, me, black Nala.
Earth, core, earth, you, black sky, black space.

PROVERB XII: THE HUNTER

The hunter in search
of an elephant
does not stop to throw
stones at birds.
It seems we don't hunt,
though, and the elephants
are long gone from this place.
The name of the hill,
Mpologoma, means lions,
but there are none; there is
no one left who remembers
the name as accurate. Your
mother away at a meeting
with the women of the
parish, you and I and the
black goat wandered out
in the pasture, past the
cows chewing in their sleep.
Out farther and farther,
almost to the house of the
muzeyi who celebrated her
hundred and third feast day
last week. I was so weary
with heat and chalk and
papers to mark, we
stopped at the edge of the pasture
and sank to the earth.
Sometime, this will all

come back to me, I fear.
There was no elephant,
there was no hunt, there
were only tinkerbirds,
palm swifts and the black goat
trilling and bleating; here
and there a honeyguide
puffed its yellow cheekfeathers
with air and sound and song—
more song, I fear, than I'll ever remember.

FIXING LIVER

My job for the farewell party was to fix the liver:
slap the thick flesh with the broad spoon;
slowly peel the membrane, and toss it
to the compost pile for the pig to eat.
Slap, peel, slap, flip—slap, peel, slap.

Cutting through the liver, making pieces to fry,
I moved the knife slowly through the meat,
holding firmly—quarter inch slices
dredged in flour, browned up crisp but
soft in the middle. "You people!" Gerald

exclaims at me when I don't eat the bits
he serves me—"Liver is lovers' food."
He must have been a big bull. Judging by
the toughness, he must have been old.
So I eat—and chew hard—and mutter,

in spite of myself as I chew, about
the butcher's kindness and the distiller's
good *tonto* (which I still only pretend
to drink). "Don't move," I tell myself.
"Don't blink." I believed, and still believe,

we were eating from a hunger
that would lead, in time, to a single,
thick memory from which I would
slowly peel the membrane, and it would
be sweet with unknowing, dredged and fading.

SOMETIMES NOW

I—without meaning to—reach my hand
to the slight curve at the low part of my
back and feel where the bones arc, where
the recessed spine becomes bow-like into flesh.

I want to know what your hands felt
as you moved them on me that evening
we walked to the far pasture and the farther well
and I came home bumpy from mosquitoes—

and on the morning you walked with me
past the primary school and the headmaster
swung his stick at the bell as we passed and
you forgot to leave your hands in your pockets;

when you felt me give to your firm encircling
of my waist, when you handled my hips
as my students handled long stanzas—
first with undue trepidation and debilitating awe

and later with energy unchecked,
beating the rhythms on their plank desktops
I was too much myself, so now I move my hands
up my back again, raising my dress a bit,

just as you would and I am privately consoled—
to move in your place, my vanilla bean,
my crushed cloves, my brief Amen.

PEOPLE ARE ALLOWED TO DO THIS

People are allowed to do this;
people are allowed to sit up all night
staring out the window at nothing visible.

People are allowed to watch
and think and not recall a purpose.
People are allowed to think and remember:

the six yards of fabric we wore,
the ground nuts we pulled for market,
staring out the window to nothing visible.

The cow from which I squeezed a cupful of milk,
the student who brought a live chicken to school.
People are allowed to do this;

to love and love a man and soak in the silence
of stunted trees and chicken-beak buttons, just as I
stare out the window to nothing visible.

People heave dry sobs of pain
that isn't personal or concrete.
People are allowed to have this

pain of missing a world you have no claim to,
pain of walking barefoot over potato mounds
and weaving a sloppy mat and coming home
to stare out the window at nothing visible

and cry into the plate of chicken and broccoli
and minute rice because it's so much, so much.
But people are allowed to do this,

people are allowed to receive paychecks
and pay electricity bills and landscape their yards
and stare out the window at nothing

but the little trickling ponds of water on
either side of the walkway.
Am I allowed to do this?

To sit at a stoplight and watch kids walk by
with pink backpacks and light-up shoes
and stare out the window and spatter

my glasses with tears again because
I know no other response.
People are allowed to stare, to think, to whisper
plaintive songs in foreign tongues to the

tiny clock set to Ugandan time.
God bless these people. We are the goats
at dusk who bleat and bleat for home.

GLOSSARY

Ayi Mukama: Lord, I praise you

Baganda: the largest tribe of Uganda (the prefix 'ba' refers to an ethnic group or people)

Bambi: A consoling word, a word of affirmation and agreement with the speaker.

Buganda: the area where the Baganda live (the prefix 'bu' refers to the land occupied by a tribe)

Bilungi: things are fine

Boda-boda man: a man on a motorcycle, bicycle, or moped who drives people around for hire on the back of his bike.

Bulungi: I am fine

Busera: a traditional grain in the central region of Uganda, used mostly for porridge

Chapats: fried dough shaped like a tortilla

Erinya lyo gwe 'ani: what is your name

Gomesi: the traditional dress for Baganda women

Gulu: a district in Northern Uganda experiencing violence and terrorism from the Kony rebels and Sudanese terrorists; literally, the word means 'heaven'

Kale: yes, ok

Kampala: the capital of Uganda

Kasekalese: he who laughs a lot

Ki, ki: hey! a casual greeting

Luganda: the language spoken by the Baganda tribe (the prefix 'lu' refers to the language spoken by a tribe or group of people)

Lugave: the clan of which my host family is a part

Luzungu: the language of white people

Mwebale: thank you for the good work

Muzungu: foreigner or white person (plural *Bazungu;* the prefix 'mu' refers to an individual)

Naruhanga: glory be to God

Nkwagala: my beloved, or, I love you

Nnaalongo: mother of twins, a title of high distinction

Nnyabo: woman, literally 'my mother,' a general greeting and way of addressing women

Oli otya: how are you

Omwana: my child, my little one

Otenderezawe: Lord, I glorify and honor you

Pichi-pichi: motorcycle

Se' mani: I don't know

Sitti cawoo: hush, don't cry

Ssaalongo: father of twins, a title of high distinction

Ssebbo: man, literally 'my master,' a general greeting and way of addressing men

Sula bulungi: sleep well

Tonto: banana beer, also called local brew

Wasuze otya: good morning, how did you sleep

Wange: what do you want from me

Waragi: a local spirit, about 70% alcohol, pronounced 'wa-lodge;' used for drinking and for fuel in the paraffin lamps

NOTES & ACKNOWLEDGMENTS

Thanks to the editors of the following magazines, where some of these poems were first published:

The Oregonian: "Gerald's Prayer in Gulu"
Portland Magazine: "Agnus Dei"
Guernica: "Kiganda Women: Secondary School (Fildah With Stanley Kunitz I)," "On Not Caning My Students," "Angel Saint"

The author would like to thank the students and teachers of Kiganda Highway Secondary School, Sister Ambrose and Sister Pascazia of St. Matia Mulumba Dispensary, Nnaalongo and Ssaalongo, Fr. Achilles Kiwanuka, and Ssemakula Gerald.

Thank you to Herman Asarnow and Lou Masson.

To Christine Muir, *mwebale nnyabo!*

I would also like to express my gratitude to my parents, Bruce and Kristy, my sister Hannah, and the rest of my family for their support and love.

Finally, thank you to Allison Rutter.